SAVING AMERICA ... FROM THE PARTIES

THE END OF THE

BEGINNING ...

OR THE BEGINNING

OF THE END?

©DONALD J. COLE, EXECUTIVE DIRECTOR
NO PARTIES AMERICA.ORG

Published   by: Century   International   Publishing   Company
10924 Grant Road, Houston, TX 77070

Created in the United States of America

ISBN 978-0-9679173-8-2

1. Current Affairs
2. Education & Teaching
3. Law
4. Political Science & Government

DEDICATION:

I dedicate this book to all American Patriots . . . who from the earliest days of our National birthing and through the more than two centuries of our history as a Nation, gave their all to create, defend and preserve this greatest Country ever raised on the earth; the beacon of freedom and justice for all the world. May the trials and sacrifices endured by all those fine American Patriots remain brightly in our minds and our hearts. May we always honor them for their great contributions by doing all we can to preserve and to serve their gift to us . . . America.

GOD BLESS AMERICA

Table of Contents

FOREWORD:

In the 1980's "Looking For Love In All The Wrong Places" was a popular country song. Recently, in the midst of a spirited political discussion among some like minded friends, that song title came to mind. The discussion focused on the perils of the present day mess the election process has become. It occurred to me that, collectively, we sounded like the singer lamenting, in song, his wrongheaded approach to finding love.

I can remember similar discussions as long as forty years ago. The subject those days often was how to cure voter apathy. My position on that *particular subject* is much the same today as it was then. As an Election Judge, at the time, I was very pleased on one occasion when a voter in my Precinct brought two visiting relatives with him to the Polls and asked me to describe our election process to them. The relatives were visiting from Australia. We had a nice visit. They learned how our election process worked and I learned from them that, in Australia in those times, every eligible voter was required to vote or face serious consequences that could be in the form of stiff fines or even jail time. I believe we should have similar requirements in America.

My position on that issue has been the source of many a heated discussion with my Republican colleagues from those long ago days until this moment. I will explain my reasoning.

Let me preface my explanation with this clarifying statement. When I embraced the concept used in Australia, forty odd years ago, we did not have, in this great country of ours, the ***extensive*** *array of corruptions in our election process that we have today*. That said, it is important that you understand that my position on the Australian method does not relate, by extension, to the many other major ills of our election process. I will address those other issues separately, later in this book.

Here is my reasoning for the Australian idea. I believe that the single most important problem we must solve in America is that *we do not have the representative government . . .The "of the people, by the people, for the people" that the founding fathers initially and, expertly, crafted*.

What we actually have today; what has evolved, or perhaps I should say "devolved", into purely and simply **"Special Interest Government"**.

Voter apathy, *lack of participation in the process by all eligible citizens is the CAUSE of the Special Interest Government EFFECT.* Voting is a privilege that ranks very high in the long list of privileges we enjoy in America.

No other people on earth . . . read that again . . .No Other People On Earth, in the entire history of the world, have enjoyed the enormous list of privileges we have in our Nation. In spite of that fact . . . *perhaps because of it*, many Americans, far too many of them, take our privileges for granted. That's a mistake that can have devastating consequences.

There is a flip side to privileges. Every privilege carries a price. The price of privilege is a complementary and *equal degree of responsibility*. When people fail or refuse to shoulder their fair share of responsibility, the privilege itself becomes tainted. At some point, the privilege might even be lost.

Today, in America, I hear the same objections about requiring every eligible voter to vote as I heard forty years ago: some of these people are too ignorant to vote; they don't understand the issues; they don't have the mental capacity to study the issues, and on and on it goes. I do not disagree with the folks who say there are some people among us who don't know - or care - what the issues are. But, I believe those people; at least many if not most of them, could be educated. They could learn how to evaluate candidates and issues well enough to vote for the people and issues they believe would be best for America, for themselves and *their families.* I also believe, very strongly, that there are numerous ways to accomplish the education of those people. I will have more to say on that issue later on. If you are wondering why I have bolded and italicized "their families", it is because those words represent a vital component of how and why our system has become so dangerously corrupted. I will address the point in detail later on.

As things now exist in what passes for our election process, various studies through many years have shown that approximately fifty percent of citizens who are **eligible** to register to vote do not **bother** to register. Those individuals **write-off their own right to vote**, as if it meant nothing. Many of those people do not register because they believe that their single vote cannot make any difference. Others are content to go with the flow and take what comes. The "go with the flow – take what comes" crowd are the ones I most despise. They are, generally, the Takers in our society, content to take what you and the rest of us produce. Still others of them don't care about anything outside their own skin and fail to understand the real threat that represents to their own well being. The bottom line is that in any given year or election cycle, approximately only fifty percent of citizens eligible to vote are **registered.** Of the total number of registered voters, in a major election, like a Presidential election, a sixty or seventy percent turnout of registered voters is considered outstanding (*why anyone would call that an outstanding performance is beyond my comprehension*). In lesser elections the turnout might be as low as ten percent or less of **registered** voters. **This is a problem of astonishing proportions.**

If, in a Presidential election, there is a seventy percent turnout, that means anything in excess of thirty-five percent of **registered** voters will decide that election. Looking closer, any number above seventeen and a half percent (**17-1/2%**) of the total number of citizens **eligible** to vote will have decided the election. **But there is worse news!** In elections for State Offices, County and Local elections, propositions and bond elections, where 10% turnouts are not particularly uncommon, slightly more than Five percent (**5%)** of those who are eligible to vote can decide those contests and issues.

Think of that! A little more than five percent of the people eligible to vote could, and often do decide the fate of important propositions that carry long term, major tax consequences, choose who will fill local, county or state offices that will decide many issues that could reach into your private life and property. If all of the above does not constitute a crisis situation, then someone will have to redefine the word crisis for me.

It *is* a crisis; a growing crisis. **And the crisis has put special interest groups in charge of your life.** The crisis and the power of the special interests will continue to grow until either the people wake up and take action to reverse the trend and **take back our Nation** or our country becomes the latest addition to the trash heap of failed societies that have piled up throughout the world's history.

The best way to ensure we have **representative government** is to have every person who is **eligible** to vote, registered and voting in every election.

I am not a Utopian, so I know that we could never achieve full participation. I also know that there must be a **learning process** to accompany any serious attempt to accomplish **substantially full participation** in the election process.

A Crisis of Conscience

The underlying basis of the crisis in our election process is a "Crisis of Conscience". The simple truth is that many Americans today have become inured to the massive array of evils that have penetrated our day to day life, the degeneration of our general society and the severe erosion of our National collective morality. Some Americans; many of them, actually, have **embraced** the evil that has invaded us, as a people.

If you do not know; never were taught or learned by your own study of our Nation's birth, that America was founded on a strong foundation of Christian religious values, principles and responsibilities, by English refugees who fled the oppression of the British Crown . . . if you do not know these things; then eligibility to vote should be withheld from you, by law, until you have learned them.

This Nation was created and rose upon the planet as a haven for People of powerful Christian beliefs to be free to practice those beliefs without any interference from the government.

The Declaration of Independence, the United States' Articles of Confederation, the United States Constitution and Bill of Rights . . . all of our Founding Documents, firmly and clearly declare those Christian beliefs and principles to be the basis of our National existence and purpose.

I write these words today, with a heavy heart and deeply troubled spirit, in the wake of the pathetic outcome of the 2012 Presidential Election. I am Heartsick and Heartbroken. America . . . at least the America that I grew up in and loved, like the devoted and faithful millions of our forebears whose vision and courage, sacrifice and suffering; and who willingly gave their own lives in the struggles to create, preserve and pass on to us, living today, this glorious Nation . . . *IS DEAD*.

The question now is: *What will replace her?* I, for one, will do everything I am capable of doing to build a *New America* and restore all of the true *American Spirit, Values and Virtues*.

As I always do in times of distress, crisis or loss, I searched my inspirational source materials for words that enlighten and comfort. I came upon the following words of Robert Browning Hamilton, which seemed to fit the occasion:

> I walked a mile with Pleasure,
> She chatted all the way,
> But left me none the wiser,
> For all she had to say.

> I walked a mile with Sorrow,
> And ne'er a word said she,
> But, oh, the things I learned from her,
> When Sorrow walked with me.

Based upon the vote counts I have seen: Obama – 59,917,178; Romney – 57,304,430; a total, between the two, of 117,275,608. (This is not the final count, but the winning margin, we are told, will remain about the same with the final count). The estimated total voting age population of America is 234.5 million Americans. Do the math and you can see that the total number of voters in the 2012 Presidential Election was approximately 50% of the total voting age (*eligible*) people. The 51% to 49% winning margin in the race for President reveals that *approximately 25.5%* of voting age Americans elected Obama to a second term. But the most troubling statistic is that *almost Fifty-Percent of voting age America*ns did not even bother to participate in the process. Yes, indeed, that is a *Crisis.*

The Crisis of Conscience is the result of the degeneration and decay of American society. From the Founding days of 1776 until the mid 1960's Americans, with few exceptions, were blessed with a conscience that guided them along the right path; the path of honor, decency and faithfulness.

In the Mid Sixties, the enemies of America and of Christianity made a breakthrough and established a beachhead in the war to destroy America **and** her Religious Institutions.

Year by year and decade by decade, America's enemies gained ground and the American People, more and more, fell into degeneracy and moral decay through such things as the "Sexual Revolution', the so-called "Women's Equal Rights" movement, the "Drug Culture", the "Free Love" movement and the American Holocaust of the so-called "Free Choice" movement, in the wake of the infamous "Roe vs. Wade" United States Supreme Court decision.

The Enemies . . . left broadly unchallenged . . . infiltrated every level of our society, our governments and, incredibly, even our Churches. The insidious changes initiated in many of our Churches and other institutions masked their real intent; that of destroying those Institutions and Churches, led us into the era of so-called "Political Correctness" which, through its numerous, devious masquerades continues to turn our men into cowering wimps and our women into treacherous predators who completely reject the God given Biblical role of woman, in the Human Family and Society in general.

Throughout that **relentless process**, we have seen an equally relentless increase in diseases of all kinds, loss of innocence in our children, soaring illegitimate childbirth rates and, at the core of it all, a loss of common decency and **abandonment of conscience** by tens of millions of Americans!

Allow me to go back to the song title that came to mind in the discussion I mentioned in the opening paragraph: "Looking For Love In All The Wrong Places". It appears to me that we persist, in America, in "Looking For Solutions In All The Wrong Places". Even worse, we are collectively closing our eyes to many of the problems themselves; never mind how to solve them. I am going to be a bit facetious here, but in addition to the song reminder, I also recall a cartoon I saw many years ago. The 'Toon depicted a large group of Ostriches scattered around a field. All but one of them had his/her head buried in the sand. That one Ostrich had his head up, looking around. The caption read: "Where'd everybody go?" Can you see any parallel here?

I contend that massive election reform, from the registration process all the way through the campaigning and election process, is urgently needed in America, and soon. I offer the thoughts in this small book to stimulate thought, discussion and action. We all must carry our weight in the management of the Republic – that's the **"By The People" part** of the system. And, it's a "use it or lose it" challenge.

Donald J. Cole
Cypress, Texas

CHAPTER ONE
KILLING THE ROOTS

The decay that has permeated our election system and continues to grow throughout that process which is vital to the continued success of the American Experiment must be eliminated completely and replaced by a system that is shielded from corruption and abuse and is dedicated to restoring and strengthening the purity of the system that the Founders worked so hard and sacrificed so much to create for Posterity.

No system of government is, or was ever, perfect. I know of no one who would claim perfection for any living human being. Nor do I believe that human beings will ever be perfect. Perfection is something we strive for but recognize, as we do, that actual perfection in ourselves or anything we do or we create, is not within the realm of possibility. Yet, we continue to strive to accomplish what is as close to real perfection as is humanly possible. Thus, we are challenged to never cease our efforts to be better and do better in all of our endeavors.

America's government, though not perfect, is and has been since its inception to the present day, the single greatest government in the history of the world, in its quest for purity, equality and individual freedom. God, our creator . . .(use whatever reference you are comfortable with to describe the Almighty) has richly showered many blessings on our Nation.

We also have, as a Nation, faced and successfully overcome many enormous difficulties and challenges to our continued existence as a Nation. We have been the Beacon of Freedom and Justice for the entire world. We have aided our earthly neighbors and raised millions from the depths of despair, disease and abject poverty, asking for nothing in return, nor boasting of our efforts to aid and comfort those with whom we share this earth.

May we never retreat from that Noble Path.

But in this time of great and growing distress throughout the world, we must address the challenge to muster the vision, the wisdom, the courage and the strength of our Founders, and the millions of American Patriots who followed them, to cure our present ills, rebuild and rededicate our Nation and our lives to the task of restoring the Beacon of Freedom we have always been and the high calling we must answer.

Our present day malaise draws its existence from a series of roots that grew out of bad seeds sown around the base of our Nation's tree of life and now threaten to overcome the original roots and our National existence.

The roots I refer to include: those of fraud, corruption, deceit, conceit, greed, avarice, immorality, treason . . . and more. We must methodically kill those destructive roots and rip them from our system. To accomplish the job, we need to reform the system from beginning to end; from top to bottom.

We have allowed the registration/voting process to become polluted to the point of stinking. There is no excuse and no justification for the present mess. What we must do to solve the problem of our severely polluted election system is dilute the toxic constituents from the process until the process is purified. Friends, that is not difficult to do.

Our present day registration system is fraught with peril and wracked with abuses. Dead people should not be voting. Convicted Felons, incarcerated in prisons, should not be voting. Illegal Aliens should not be voting. I know, for a fact, from personal experience in conducting post election vote audits that such violations occur regularly. No person should have more than one voter registration card, or find it possible in any way to cast more than a single vote in any election. Yet, every one of the conditions above exists today in our system, and in alarming numbers in some areas. And, yes, I will say that much of said voter fraud is condoned . . . even sponsored by elements of the Parties. I leave it to you to decide which Party or Parties that is. Whether or not we adopt a policy requiring all eligible citizens to vote, our election process, especially our registration process is compromised and absolutely must be repaired.

Starting with the voter registration mess, we must then continue on through Party reform, Campaign reform, Elections reform. When the system reform, from Registration, to Party, to Campaign, to Elections is completed, there are many more reforms that we need to see, including: Bureaucracy, Tax, Welfare, Military, Judicial, and Immigration reforms, not necessarily in that order. This book does not address these additional areas that need attention, but focuses on the Registration through Election Cycle.

The elements of the process to reform and repair the system of Elections in America must be all-inclusive, addressing every aspect, from the Registration process, through the Campaigning components, including impacts to the system of practices and activities from any quarter, public or private and through the actual Election itself.

CHAPTER TWO
VOTER REGISTRATION

The first action, to get the total reform process underway should be to declare a **National Voter Registration Period**; say a three or four month duration, during which every voter in every state is required to register anew under specific new minimum guidelines that, once met, would permit any voter of any state, under the new system, to vote in any **National** Election. The **Primary Requirement** for every citizen to obtain registration would be to appear, in person, before a Registration Board official and show documentary **proof of United States Citizenship.** Failure to provide the required documentary proof of U.S. Citizenship would render the individual **ineligible** to vote in **any election (Federal, State or Local),** until such time that the individual was able to present, in person, the required proof to the Registration Board.

In the case of sick, elderly, or otherwise handicapped individuals who would be unable to personally appear at the Registration Board, accommodations would be available to those individuals to have a Registration Board official **visit such individuals at their place of residence.** Other accommodations would be employed to make in-person registration available to Ex-Patriot Americans working abroad, Diplomats, Military personnel and such other U.S. citizens working and stationed outside of the United States.

Looking back to the discussion in this book's Foreword concerning any refinements in *defining the parameters for "eligibility"*. Those components, as well, would be part of the New Registration Process. Each of the States could, *at its own discretion, directed by the voters of that State, impose additional criteria for its registered voter citizens to establish and/or maintain eligibility to vote in State or local elections within that State. (e.g. require voters to be property owners and show proof of ownership, to be eligible to vote in any bond election).* No voter in any State would be permitted to vote in any election without, first having satisfied the requirements to establish *proof of U. S. Citizenship*.

The best way to ensure that we have representative government is to have every person who is eligible to vote, registered and voting in every election. As previously stated, I am not a Utopian, and know that we could never achieve full participation. I know, also, that there must be a *learning process* to accompany any serious attempt to accomplish *full participation* in the election process.

What I do not accept, at face value, is the often heard argument that some people are "too stupid", "too uninformed", or "otherwise unfit" to vote. Allow me to state in the clearest language I can: If we are at the point . . . or can ever conceive of reaching a point in America, where there is anything remotely approaching a number of citizens who are "too stupid", "too ignorant", "too otherwise unfit" to vote that would constitute more than a very small fraction of the voters, when every eligible voter voted . . . then we are far worse off than I could ever comprehend. That notion, my friends, is a myth that BOTH of the Parties would like you to believe. It is insulting to anyone of normal intelligence. I do not buy it . . . and neither should you.

But keep in mind that the operative word is *"eligible"*. The process of changing to a requirement that every "eligible" voter must vote would certainly involve revisiting and revamping the parameters that *define eligibility*. In the early days of our Republic, one had to be a *property owner* to be eligible to vote. For many decades, *women were not eligible to vote*.

The issue of an individual's fitness to be eligible to vote is a legitimate point for discussion and definition. But the *Discussing and Defining*, in order to be true to the concept of government "Of the People, By the People and For the People", must be *conducted* of, by and for the People . . . *all of the people*.

In order to establish and codify the parameters necessary to determine fitness and eligibility to vote in National Elections, a Commission, consisting of learned individuals, prominent in their fields of expertise, such as, Medicine, Law, etc., should be established to study the issue and make recommendations

I want to offer a few words here about the family's role in elections and its relevance to the registration process. You recall that I bolded and italicized *"their families"* in the Foreword,

Regarding the views held by some that certain people are too stupid or too dumb, etc. to vote "intelligently". I refuse to accept such a false notion. They are people . . . Americans . . . Taxpayers, with families to support. They have dreams and needs and Rights. They know what they want for their families . . . and for their Country. They may be wrong about some things, but they have a Right to be wrong. Perhaps they are not scholars; So, What!

An astonishing number of great men and women rose from extremely humble beginnings. That condition will always be part of the human condition. And their Rights . . . you know . . . those inalienable gifts they are endowed with by God . . .are not contingent upon intelligence or scholarship. Some of the most ignorant people I've ever encountered, during my more than three quarters of a century of life in this Country, accumulated most of their **utter stupidity**, I believe, in the pursuit of the Advanced Degrees they hold.

One of my greatest concerns about our Nation in these treacherous times, and that of many others I know all over America, is the **proliferation of attacks on the family** . . . the foundation and building block of our civilized society . . . by the evildoers in our midst, who work to destroy us. "The Family" must be protected, defended and preserved. Oh, how America has changed for the worst. I recall from my childhood in the war years of WWII that there were merchants discovered, occasionally, who were charging outrageous prices for scarce goods. When discovered, they were labeled as "Profiteers" and became Pariahs in their communities – **outcasts!** Today, those Pariahs would more likely be labeled in the stupid vernacular of the present day as "rock stars."

The "evildoers" I have referenced must also be looked at in the establishment of an eligibility matrix. We will always have people among the general population who are ne'er-do-wells, radicals, rebels . . . misfits of various types. Perhaps certain sub-sets of those various types would be classified as unsuitable and proposed to be **ineligible voters**. Then, that recommendation would become one of the items on the referendum for the National Vote.

The Commission should have a specific period of time in which to conduct its studies and make its recommendations to the People, after which all currently registered voters would have the opportunity to vote in a National referendum that would establish all of the legal parameters that would be required to establish registration eligibility for all future National Elections. Such parameters might include: e.g. U.S. Citizenship, Certified Mental Incapacity, Stability or Sanity, Minimum Age, Criminal History and any other factors identified by the Commission, included in their recommendations and adopted by a majority or, perhaps a super-majority vote on the referendum.

A second National Voter Registration Period would follow the passage and enactment of the standards for voter registration eligibility, within one month after the formal adoption of standards that passed in the referendum.

An individual's failure to meet a particular established parameter for registration eligibility, e.g. an individual living in a medically confirmed permanent vegetative state would be cause to deny registration. Any such individual would have the right to legally appeal or challenge such determination.

CHAPTER THREE
ELIMINATE THE PARTY PROCESS

A number of the Founding Fathers, George Washington and John Adams among them, opposed the Party System, believing it would have a divisive effect. The extreme polarization of the two major Parties today; The Republican Party and The Democrat Party, gives weight to President Washington's and President Adams' belief. We see, today, the *failed* Party System they wisely envisioned more than two centuries in the past.

With the Republican and Democrat Parties being the two major Parties in America, many people in our society refer to our system as a "Two Party System". That, of course, is not an accurate statement. The existence of other "minor" Parties, though it is played down in most quarters, can be a major influence in the outcome of an election.

Elections in recent history have shown that to be true. When a minor Party candidate siphons off enough votes from one of the Major Party candidates it can cause that candidate to lose the election to the other Major Party candidate. Generally a substantial minor Party candidate will take a significant number of votes away from only one of the Major Party candidates.

The likelihood of a minor Party candidate actually winning an election is quite remote. In practice, minor Party candidates, campaign rhetoric aside; usually only fill the role of "Spoiler" to one of the Major Party candidates. Minor Party Candidates, also often have a hidden agenda and an equally hidden ulterior motive for running. Typically, as well, they are usually running against only one of the Major Party Candidates

Nevertheless, these minor Parties that spring up from time to time; usually only to disappear in a few years or less, *consume*, just as the two Major Parties do, substantial (though lesser) amounts of resources: time and money.

Resources; the precious components that drive the engine of progress and prosperity, come in many varieties. There is an extraordinary array of natural resources, some finite, some renewable. Man-made resources, everything from refined products, such as oil and gasoline, to steel, textiles, food products, pharmaceuticals; time and money are also part of the total range of resources.

In order to preserve and protect our American way of life and our world leadership position, we must use all of our resources wisely; judiciously. I contend that for far too long we have squandered resources, in ever-increasing amounts, on the Party System of electing and mis-managing our government. Allow me to illustrate:

Hundreds of millions of dollars, perhaps billions, along with millions of man-hours are expended in every election cycle to do nothing more than support the Party Process. Not one cent of those dollars, or one minute of those hours does anything to support National Defense, or to increase our Gross Domestic

Product or improve our Balance of Trade with the world. Instead, the Party System continues to grow and use up more and more resources we would be far better off using to produce goods and services to be sold in the marketplace for profit.

Consider with me for a moment the positive, powerful impact on our National economy and standard of living if those hundreds of millions, or billions, of dollars, in each four year election cycle, were put to better, productive use. I mentioned textiles above among man made resources we use. Think about the number of textile mills that have closed in America in the last few decades, replaced by mills in foreign countries. Think about the ***thousands of jobs that Americans lost in that process, not great paying jobs, perhaps, but decent paying jobs that supported families*** . . . lost to lower paid foreign workers.

Now reflect on how different the picture would be if, instead of pouring hundreds of millions, or billions, into the proliferation of political Party Waste, those dollars had been spent on ***higher quality U.S. textile products and wages*** for the ***American people*** who made them, and the ***American salesmen and women*** who sold them to ***American consumers*** at higher prices than cheap, imported goods, produced by ***"foreign slave labor".***

And, now, spend a little time with your own imagination (with a side glance into your conscience) and see how many scenarios you can develop to illustrate how much better the enormous use of resources, time and money currently ***wasted on perpetuating the failed Party System***, could be invested in

America's productivity and prosperity. One needn't be a Rhodes Scholar to see the enormous positive potential.

There is also something else that my mind is wrestling with more and more with the passage of time. Have you paid any attention at all to the vanishing Middle Class American? Like those thousands of Textile Mill workers who were once Middle Class Americans but now find themselves at or below the so-called Poverty Level?

Have you ever conjured up a notion in your mind, as I have, that the Parties (whether they have a carefully constructed plan to systematically accomplish the end result, or not) are steadily moving along a path that will end in the total elimination of the Middle Class? Would the Parties benefit from the complete elimination of the Middle Class? It is something to think about and watch very carefully.

The Party System is an increasing drain on our resources and a cancer on our election process. The Party System has degenerated to the point that we have Toxic Polarization with obscene amounts of time, money and resources feeding both sides. The time has come to recognize the wisdom of those Founders, like Washington, Adams and others of their contemporaries who counseled against such a flawed System. Those great men understood the danger that was and is in the Party System that has so *grievously damaged our society and our National Integrity*. By the very nature of its structure, the Party System works to *destroy Unity; to Divide and to Weaken us as a great Nation.*

We hear a great deal today about *"Diversity"*. The misuse of that word, like other words in our lexicon, has been adopted by certain factions and groups and has been very effectively used as a tool for political purposes. It galls me to hear some of the Captains of Industry and most Career Politicians rhapsodize over the word "Diversity". One might rightly wonder if those individuals are immersed in some sort of deep religious experience or ritual. "Diversity"? ***Talk about being focused on the wrong thing!*** I challenge anyone to show me any great accomplishment; any great achievement that was reached by the application of "Diversity"! The Party System relies heavily on Diversity. The Parties desperately need Diversity to thrive, survive and grow. But BEWARE! As the Parties thrive, survive and grow . . . the Republic gradually dies.

What we desperately need in these present times "that try men's souls" is **UNITY!** Every great thing ever accomplished by our Nation or any other Body of People, was accomplished as a result of "Unity". Allow me to express another example of misuse, frequently used by both of the Major Parties.

Have you ever heard some Politician say "we must do this or that", or perhaps "we did this or that . . . to Unite the Party", or "to Unify the Party"? I have heard many variations of that over my lifetime. But, ***hold on a minute!*** What does that rhetoric (Drivel) really mean in terms of what is good for America? If the Democrats or the Republicans engage in "uniting" the Party, what is it that they are uniting for? The simple answer is: "for the good of the Party". That, in turn, translates to: "to the detriment of the other Party". The real tragedy in all of that is

28

that they "unite" the Party or Parties in order to **DIVIDE** the Nation. Friends I am not now, nor have I ever been, a Rocket Scientist. But, I maintain that one needn't be a Rocket Scientist to be able to see and understand the dangers and the threats to a Unified Nation . . . a United States of America . . . in the *failed Party System*.

Looking even closer at the down side of a Party System, consider carefully that a Party System that, necessarily pits one group against the other, appeals to man's baser instincts that come in the form of conceit, greed, selfishness, dishonesty, immorality and a host of other evils the we have all seen clearly demonstrated in all of the "Parties".

Is "More of the same . . . Only worse" what you want for our Nation . . . your grandchildren , or Posterity? Isn't it time for us, as citizens of the world's greatest Nation to accept our responsibility and fix the mess that we have allowed to happen? You Can! I Can! All of us Can! . . . together, *United in the true Spirit of our Beloved Land*. We need to get back to our roots, to our fundamental Founding Values. *The Party System must end. Now!*

CHAPTER FOUR
CURTAIL THE CAMPAIGN TRAIL

"What's Past Is Prologue", the saying goes. There's plenty of truth in Mr. Shakespeare's little four word bit of wisdom from his play "The Tempest". The words have been around for a long time and there are multiple interpretations of the actual meaning of them. Allow me a brief comment.

First, it is important to know that those words, much bandied about down through the ages, were followed by these words: "what to come, in yours and my discharge". The Prologue . . . in a play . . . the past, which has already been presented . . . has already happened, thus the Prologue of the play, as Antonio explains to Sebastian, simply sets the stage for the great things that are to come in their "discharge", that is in their hands, and the things that will make them great. Thus, the common use of the phrase to indicate that what we've seen before is what we can expect to see again and again, is a bit off the mark.

I drafted the above commentary in the days leading up to the November 6, 2012 National Election; the days nearing the end of the Prologue, which now an accomplished historical event. If the future, as we move past the end of the Prologue, repeats itself (the notion that most people believe to be the meaning of the quote "What's Past is Prologue") we will likely see just more and more of the same tired, worthless drivel from our government, our politicians and the massive assortment of worthless hangers on and scammers (that my eighth grade teacher would have labeled "excess baggage").

However, **taking a different perspective with a more positive focus**, I believe we have before us, an **opportunity,** one more in line with the real meaning of the much used and misunderstood Shakespearean quote!

We can join together in the **true spirit of America** and take charge of **our responsibilities and our opportunities! We can, as a People, do great and different things** that will greatly benefit our lot and our future. **Yes, we can indeed** . . . if we, as individuals, come together . . . **Unite** . . . and resolve to stop the bleeding and improve our National condition.

I contend that our ongoing, what can best be called **addiction** to, the four years long, National election campaigns that have become an integral part of the American Political Landscape, is a major component of the **gradual, persistent destruction of the Republic.**

Can any thinking person fail to see the record of enormous damage that has already been done to the whole of our election process by the corrupted **campaign** process? Think about it for a moment . . . no, better yet, for a day, or a week, or a month. Study the effect these endless campaign seasons have had. Investigate the scams, the dirty tricks, the confusion and corrupt products that have oozed out of the seeming perpetual campaign practice and its powerfully **negative impact on our American way.**

I do not hold myself up and present myself to you as a prophet. I am not a prophet, with mystical powers of extrasensory perception. Rather, I am simply an American Patriot . . . not the "summer soldier and sunshine Patriot" that

Thomas Payne called attention to in December 1776 . . . and we are, once again, facing "the times that try men's souls". *We cannot go on forever abusing the great creation of our Founders and expect that creation and our way of life to survive and prosper.*

If you study the campaign process even briefly; you cannot fail to see what it has become. The **attacks**, the lies and misrepresentations, media manipulation, errors, omissions, false charges, ignored facts and much more rage on for months and years, creating the exact opposite of what a political campaign should be. A campaign should serve to inform; to provide factual information and details of the candidates, the factual issues, the positions of the candidates and all possible factual, relevant peripheral data about the candidates and the issues.

In these present times that, indeed, do "try men's souls", our campaign system, our news media, the Parties, the Candidates and campaign staffs, the Pollsters, Lobbyists and countless other hangers-on and assorted other special interest participants have become so degraded and disgraced that, taken as a whole, they constitute a **toxic blend** of all that can go wrong with a system . . . **and has.**

I believe that, of greatest importance, the entire campaign process must be abbreviated; condensed to a **radically** shorter period of time, immediately preceding the Primary and Election. New rules must be developed, promulgated and enforced. The lies, deceit and criminal mischief must be eradicated to the greatest possible extent.

CHAPTER FIVE
A NEW AND BETTER PROCESS

The New Process

- Dismantle all Political Parties.
- All Candidates for election run independently with no Party Organization affiliation.
- Each candidate is allowed to establish a campaign committee or organization to develop strategies and manage the candidate's campaign. The campaign organizations may be organized and commence operations *three months in advance of the Primary Day* voting and may continue operations, within established guidelines for such considerations as Campaign Funding practices and limitations and related issues (TBD), for as long as the candidate remains as an active candidate and, if elected on Election Day, for a period of *one month after Election Day*.
- As many Eligible candidates who wish to run for an office may do so. There is no limit on the number of eligible candidates who may present themselves for an office, to run for that office in the Primary Day voting.
- The two candidates who receive the highest number of votes for any Office on Primary Day will be certified as the two candidates who will run for the Office on Election Day.

- The Electoral College will remain in place in Presidential Elections and will function as it does today. As is done today, the Electoral College will convene, after the election, and Electors from every State will cast their votes for the winning candidate from their respective states [1].
- State and Local Primaries for all offices will be conducted in the same manner as described above, with, possibly, certain State specific differences, if State voters so choose.
- Initiatives, Bond Elections and all such similar matters will appear on the ballot on Election Day, as they do at the present time.

Term Limits:

Any program for election reform should include provision for discussion of Term limits. Term Limits for State offices within a particular State, must be determined solely by the voters of the particular State. However, Term Limits for all National Offices, President/Vice-President, United States Senators and Congressmen could be, and I believe, should be part of the Election reform, with the stated position that all States would have, subsequently, at their own option, the right to enact, or not enact, State and local Term Limits by means of whatever method the particular State might choose to employ

Polling:

<u>BAN POLLING!</u> No Polling concerning any Election for National Office would be permitted by any organization for any purpose. Polling has become a major component of the poisoning of the well in the election process in America. Polling serves Special Interests; organizations and groups interested in creating or swaying opinions and perceptions . . . or, perhaps more accurately, misperceptions. Political Polling, as it exists today is simply "influence peddling" in disguise and is employed mostly to disguise issues and confuse, rather than inform the voters.

Polling organizations, large and small, can and sometimes do conduct polls for the sole purpose of creating, rather than measuring trends and opinions. Polling, it may be argued, provides allegedly valuable information to candidates and Parties about any number of conditions. It is probably true that Polling could provide such benefits to Parties and/or Candidates. But the record over the years since polling has become such a large component of what is today's election process shows that there are far too many abuses and inaccuracies that can and have been used by unscrupulous individuals to create detrimental impacts on the election process and, in some cases, the outcome of certain elections.

I contend that Polling provides no true benefits to anyone but the special interests, be they political organizations, industry organizations, labor organizations, media outlets and others, but no true benefit to the voters of this Nation.

Note[1]:

Though the Electoral College would remain, certain refinements would be made to the process of determination of the number of Electors from each State and the formula that would be used to determine the number.

AFTERWORD:

It should be obvious to the reader that I am a Conservative American Patriot who loves his Country. A Catholic American of Irish descent, I was born into a family of Democrats in Brooklyn, New York. I am the sole member of my extended family . . . siblings, parents, uncles and aunts, cousins and grandparents . . . who was not a registered Democrat. With all of my flaws and shortcomings, the Good Lord spared me that one.

A voter still had to be twenty-one years of age to be eligible to vote when, in November 1956, I voted in my first election, a year after completing my U.S. Navy service. I was a registered republican and voted for President Eisenhower for his second term, as did my wife who, like me, came from a family of Democrats (in Texas).

We were married in Brooklyn, New York, had all three of our children there and stayed for six years, until we *escaped back to Texas* in 1961. During our New York years, we were "The Republicans" in our Brooklyn District. When we moved to Texas, we found that we were "The other Republicans" in our Corpus Christi District.

Very active in politics, after our move back to Texas, I worked in a wide variety of capacities to help build the Republican Party in Texas and particularly in Houston/Harris County. The Party grew and became strong. I helped convert many of my "Conservative Democrat" friends to the Republican Party by convincing them that it was not possible to be both Conservative and Democrat. There actually was a time in our history when one *could* be *Conservative* and Democrat.

But that was before the Democrat Party changed its stripes and became what it is, in my view and that of many others today, the Progressive Socialist Party with distinct Marxist leanings; a party that continues to call itself the Democrat Party. I would call that an Oxy-Moron; but, what the heck, it's their Party (until we abolish the failed Party System and there no longer are any Parties) and we are a free country, so let them call it whatever they like.

One of my "Conservative" Democrat pals (and a fellow Catholic) whom I was able to convert to the Republican Party, actually went on to serve two terms as Texas State Republican Party Chairman, and a good one, before being term limited out.

As the Republican Party in Texas and elsewhere grew in numbers and strength, though, I began to see a trend that was very troubling to me. It appeared that the more the Republican Party grew, the more like the Democrats it seemed to become. This marked the beginning of my personal awakening to the destructive natures of the Party System. We are long past the time when I concluded, by and large, that there's not much

37

difference in the career Politicians on either side of the aisle, though I do still see a difference between the two Parties.

The problem , for me, is that, as I see it, the "Party System" has deteriorated into what I consider to be a cesspool of opportunistic leeches who, "frankly, my dear don't give a damn" about the voters: the People whom they are supposed to be working for.

The Special Interest Monster that passes today as our government has grown to unsustainable dimensions. In short . . . The System Stinks and the Well has been Poisoned. If we are to survive and continue to flourish as a Nation . . . *and I firmly believe we will,* we need to get busy at righting and repairing the Ship of State.

I write this small book in the hope of teasing you into action and with the belief that there are enough true American Patriots among our numbers who will rise to the challenge and help in the work ahead to restore America's tried and true greatness. In fact, I am counting on this little book to get the ball rolling. The challenge to us is enormous and complex. We are going to have to find new blood; good men and women who will put America ahead of themselves and serve us as Senators and Congressmen and women, Cabinet members and Federal Court Justices and, when their terms are completed, go back home to their careers and occupations in Business, Commerce, Medicine, Science or whatever is their chosen field and help build our standard of living and quality of life. That was the vision, the intent and the plan our Founders had for this Nation; this Republic. But we drifted away and now must find innovative solutions to the problems we created by our inattention to duty and our own selfishness.

God, Country and Duty must (and I believe will) become the **New Normal**. This Nation, through the Colonists' blood, sweat, tears, determination and courage had to face down and defeat the most powerful Nation then on earth, in a long and bloody war to survive the birth.

Other wars, such as the War of 1812 followed and took a heavy toll in order to preserve our existence.

The 1860's saw us at war once again . . . amongst ourselves; for years, and perilously close to self-destruction. But, again, we survived and healed.

In 1941, the Japanese Empire, with its insane, evil intent to destroy America and dominate the world, attacked us at Pearl Harbor, Hawaii. It was a sneak attack, on a quiet Sunday morning, as people were resting in their homes or attending Church services. The attack awakened the Sleeping Giant which, four years later *Ate The Japanese Dragon*. The Japanese Empire was reduced to humiliating, total defeat and signed the formal surrender documents on the Deck of the American Battleship U.S.S. Missouri, lying at anchor in Tokyo Bay. It is important to note here that, in testimony to America's greatness, we then *helped the Japanese rebuild their country*. America is well known for the kindness we show to defeated enemies who had set out to destroy us.

Today, we are at a crossroads once again, and once again, we appear to be bent upon self-destruction, as we seemed to be, leading up to the Civil War between the States.

Can we, once more, survive the dangers and sacrifices needed to restore our honor and our faith . . . and resume our High Calling?　　*Yes, we can. Yes, we must. Yes, we will!*

I am personally committed to do all that I can find it in my power to do to save and restore America. To that end, I am engaged in an effort to build a Grass-Roots, Advocacy Organization to help get the job done. ***"No Parties America.Org"*** is presently in the formative stage. The formal launch date has not yet been established, but will be announced in the near future.

My book, "The Party's Over", will be released to coincide with the launch of No Parties America.Org. In three sections: "The Problems", "The Particulars" and "The Solutions", the book will cover all of the ground in its twenty-one chapters including issues, such as: The Global Agenda, The Illegal Alien Invasion, The Open Borders Threat to National Security, The Attack on Judeo-Christian Foundations, The Specter of "I-F" (Islamo-Fascism), Bureaucracy Reform, Welfare reform, Judicial Reform, and much more. ***It all begins with the dismantling of the Party System and the election process reforms that must accompany that.*** God Bless You and God Bless America.

Donald J. Cole, August 15, 2013

Cypress, Texas

www.ingramcontent.com/pod-product-compliance
Lightning Source LLC
Chambersburg PA
CBHW060703280326
41933CB00012B/2281